The following is an adaptation of one of the Twelve Steps in the program of Overeaters Anonymous. It is one person's interpretation and does not speak for the O.A. organization.

Waking up

A new member of Overeaters Anonymous remarked at a meeting that the last ten years were little more than a blur in her memory. Since compulsive overeating had taken over her life (round-the-clock food consumption was the rule rather than the exception), other than eating she was hardly aware of what she had done during those years.

Not all of us have suffered so severely from food abuse, but we all know what happens when eating gets out of control, and we see where we are headed if left to our own devices.

Fortunately, there is an answer, a means of arresting the destructive habit of compulsive overeating. The Twelve Steps which have led so many to recovery from other kinds of addictive behavior — gambling, drinking, drug using — these same steps offer a new life to those of us who are powerless over food.

Because we were desperate, because we could not find a way out of our problems alone, and because we saw miracles of recovery occurring in the lives of others, we decided to reach for help from a power greater than ourselves. Gradually, we began to be aware of this Higher Power in the

O.A. group, in the events of every day, and deep in the quiet of our own hearts. The steps of the program have taken us through surrender, self-examination, willingness to let go of our own character defects, and the sincere attempt to make amends where needed in order to improve our relationships with other people. Each step brings us into closer contact with the God of our understanding, and we begin to wake up physically, emotionally, and spiritually.

Abstinence from the kind and quantity of food that was slowly but surely destroying us means that we can feel good physically. After an abstinent day, we can wake up the next morning alert and alive, with an inner joy. We start experiencing emotions again which had been suppressed by eating excess calories.

Our bodies and emotions have new life and so does our spirit. The longer we are around this program, the more firmly we believe that the spiritual awakening is what triggers all of the improvements. There simply is no other explanation. Sometimes the awakening happens suddenly; more often it is a gradual process.

"Having had a spiritual awakening as a result of these Steps ..."* That says a lot. We may spend the rest of our lives discovering just how much. Waking up to who we really are and becoming aware of our relationship with a Higher Power is a gift. Our part is becoming ready to receive the gift, and in order to be ready we work the steps.

A spiritual awakening does not occur on demand, but there are things we can do in preparation. We can contact other people who demonstrate a spiritual strength in their lives. We can have an open mind, a "willing suspension of disbelief,"

***Alcoholics Anonymous,** published by A.A. World Services, New York, N.Y., p. 60. Available through Hazelden Educational Materials.

if we tend to be cynical about whatever our intellects alone cannot probe. If we have been preoccupied with material needs and desires, we can wake up to the fact that we may have been missing something!

A spiritual awakening may come when we are bored and feel suffocated by our unsuccessful attempts to satisfy our physical cravings. We can see that it is a dead end road, and if we are receptive to trying an alternate route, other travelers can show us a new way that will take us where we want to go, and become our spiritual guides.

Waking up is full of surprises. We realize that many of our old ideas have become excess baggage, and we decide to get rid of them. We find that we are better off without some of the people we thought we needed. We discover that we are tuned in to individuals we formerly did not understand. Because we are linked to a new source of strength, we can lay old fears to rest and pick up new options, risks, and responsibilities. When we accept the challenge which the life of the spirit offers, we find answers to boredom and emptiness. Days which used to pass in a blur of overeating are sharply defined by new activity and experiences. The spiritual awakening attested to in Step Twelve is a quiet internal revolution which gently propels us into a new state of consciousness; we become new people.

Sharing the wealth

Perhaps the most important message of our program is that we cannot keep it unless we give it away. According to the "Big Book" (as adapted for O.A.), "Practical experience shows that nothing will so much insure immunity from (compulsive overeating) as intensive work with other (compulsive overeaters.)"*

Carrying the message to other compulsive overeaters and sharing the new life we find in O.A. are ways of giving service, and at the same time continuing our own growth and recovery. When we work with a newcomer, we hear and see ourselves as we used to be. We are reminded of who we are and where we came from. When we tell someone else about the program, we reinforce our own conviction of its importance in our lives. Active participation in meetings and frequent telephone contacts with other members keep strength and support circulating among us. When we are working the steps, we are walking examples of the program in action. The example we present says more than any number of words:

> "Life will take on new meaning. To watch people recover, to see them help others, to watch loneliness vanish, to see a fellowship grow up about you, to have a host of friends — this is an experience you must not miss ... Frequent contact with newcomers and with each other is the bright spot of our lives."*

---

*Ibid, p. 89.

We can share our program with other interested people by providing literature, listings of area meetings, and by offering to take them with us when we go to meetings.

Basically, ours is a program of attraction rather than promotion, and it is not for everyone. If your enthusiasm for O.A. is met with skepticism, you can assume that the other person is not ready to hear about the program. At the very least, you will have planted a seed, and who knows when it may bear fruit? You will have done your part in carrying the message, whether or not it is favorably received.

It is true that those of us who have experienced that pain of compulsive overeating feel a tremendous amount of empathy for those who still suffer from the illness. We've been there. We know what it's like. We can offer our understanding, insight, and support, but we cannot force the program on anyone else, regardless of how much we think that person needs it.

It is well to be aware at the outset that some of our Twelfth Step work will seem futile and frustrating. Along with all of our other efforts, we turn the results of this step over to a Higher Power. The input is our responsibility; the outcome is not.

Sometimes we may be reluctant to talk about O.A. with people who are not familiar with the program. Are we embarassed about labeling ourselves as compulsive overeaters? Are we hesitant to talk about a Higher Power and the spiritual aspects of the program?

How were you introduced to O.A.? Did you embrace the program immediately, or was there a period of time required before you were convinced that O.A. could help you? How grateful are you for hearing about it? It is the joy and gratitude we feel for at last having a solution to our number-one problem which is contagious and which prompts us to spread the good news.

Often, the people whom our Higher Power puts in our path are those with whom we share our program. If we are alert to receive the signals that come to us every day, there will undoubtedly be many opportunities to help others and thus sustain our own recovery. We can put ourselves in situations which guarantee such opportunities — meetings, for example. Do you make an effort to talk to newcomers? To exchange phone numbers? To share on an increasingly deep and meaningful level with your program friends?

Each of us has a unique story to tell. As we come out of our isolation, we can pass on the benefits of our individual experiences. Those who need to hear our story will recognize themselves when we tell it. Since we were unable to recover from compulsive overeating by ourselves, contributing to the strength of the group is what insures continued recovery for us all.

Sponsorship

After we have been around the O.A. program for a while, someone may ask us to be their sponsor. Even though we may feel inadequate for such a responsibility, Step Twelve suggests that we agree; sponsorship is part of carrying the message.

As a sponsor, we can help a new member by listening to their daily food plan, offering encouragement, and making suggestions for maintaining abstinence. We may be asked to be a program sponsor, giving guidance with the steps. Or our sponsorship may combine all elements of the program — help with physical abstinence, plus support and guidance for emotional and spiritual growth.

Honestly sharing what has happened to us and what has worked for us is our gift to make available to whoever asks for our help. In the process, we will have the satisfaction not only of making a valuable contribution, but also of being more fully known and understood by someone else. We will strengthen our own abstinence and open up new directions for our personal growth in the program.

Together we can do what we cannot do alone. We all struggle with the tendency to overeat, some of us every day and many times a day. When we make suggestions to someone else, we are reminding ourselves of what we need to do in order to remain abstinent. When we know that a newcomer is looking to us for direction and guidance, we are inspired to set a good example. A phone call helps the sponsor as much as it helps the caller.

You can only share what you have. Someone chooses you as a sponsor because you have something that person wants and needs — abstinence, a measure of serenity, a well-adjusted attitude. You share the program as it works for you. The person you are sponsoring is free to take or reject what you give. If the relationship becomes a problem for either of you, you are each free to terminate it. In the Twelve Step programs, principles are more important than personalities.

If you do not have a sponsor, why not get one? Those of us who decide that we no longer need a sponsor's help after a certain amount of time in O.A. are ignoring a vital ingredient of the program. We can each profit tremendously from a continuing close relationship with someone who knows our history, and has been with us through the ups and downs of our recovery.

When you have benefited from the time and attention of a friend and sponsor who has been patient and helpful with your efforts to maintain abstinence and follow the steps, you can pass along that same patient assistance to another compulsive overeater. That's the way the program works.

Practicing the principles

Think back to the person you were when you took Step One. How have you changed? How has your life changed? To what extent have the principles of the Twelve Step program influenced your thoughts and behavior?

"To practice these principles in all our affairs" is, of course, an ideal for which we strive, knowing that we will never perfectly achieve it. Some days we feel the satisfaction of making progress. Other days we may appear to be temporarily losing ground. What the program gives us is a framework for actions, decisions, and plans — a goal to aim for, even though we may miss it at times. The principles gradually become part of our personalities and, because they work, they have a marked influence on how we think and act each day.

Take honesty, for example. For most of us, the realization

and admission that we were powerless over food, and that our lives were a mess was the beginning of a new honesty — honesty first with ourselves and, as a result, honesty with other people.

Being honest with ourselves and our sponsor about what we are eating is a necessary ingredient of abstinence. Being honest with ourselves and the important others in our lives about our feelings and behavior is necessary for maintaining inner peace and meaningful relationships. Since we are accepted in O.A. just as we are, we don't need to fake anything.

From the experience of at last being ourselves, we realize the self-destructiveness of pretense and deception. We usually end up getting along much better with everyone when we stop falsifying ourselves in order to do what we think will please someone else.

Another of the principles that can profoundly affect us at a very deep level of our being is that of consciously turning over situations beyond our control — letting go and letting God. We start out by turning over our inability to control what we eat. From that beginning, we decide to relinquish more and more of our frustrations as we experience the relief and joy that come from learning to trust a Higher Power.

Turning over what we cannot handle does not mean that we passively do nothing and expect God to do everything for us. We do as much as we can — for example, we write down a food plan, make telephone calls, go to meetings, search for a job if we're out of work, do our part to make relationships run smoothly, look for opportunities to be of service. We do what we can, but we trust a Higher Power to take care of the outcome.

The growing confidence which we experience from turning over the unmanageable aspects of our life and finding answers causes those around us to notice a difference. "What happened to you? You seem very relaxed and happy." How you respond is your decision, but remember — you have been given a priceless gift. The only strings attached are that you share it.

Courage, humility, love, patience, acceptance — the continued development of these and other assets, along with continued abstinence from compulsive overeating, is contingent on our daily spiritual condition. If any one principle can be said to underly all of the Twelve Steps, it is perhaps that of seeking and maintaining close contact with a power greater than ourselves. If we stay in touch with the God of our understanding throughout the events of each day, we cannot go far wrong.

Practicing the principles means that we do what we need to do in order to abstain from compulsive overeating and live in harmony with ourselves and those around us. It means that we allow others to think their own thoughts, feel their own feelings, and live their own lives. It means that we are honest at home and on the job, as well as in an O.A. meeting. It means that we do not spend a lot of time and energy worrying about whether or not the sky is going to fall. It means that we go out of our way to give help, because we have been helped. It means that we swallow our pride and apologize when we have made a mistake and hurt someone else. Best of all, practicing the principles of the Twelve Step program means that life takes on new meaning and new joy.

Living today

Months and years can run together and be lost in the stupor of overeating. When we take away the anesthetic of excess calories, we come alive to the realities of the present, including the sharp edges of emotions which we were trying to dull. One day at a time, we are learning to cope with the bad feelings, the good feelings, and the in-between blahs. The message which is yours and mine to share with other compulsive overeaters is that we can live each day without excess food, provided we concentrate on **today,** now, this moment.

Yes, there is life after abstinence. It is an existence filled with new sensations, new experiences, perhaps new fears, but also new hope and new faith. What was once unmanageable can be handled one day at a time with the help of the program and a Higher Power.

When you were overeating, how much time did you spend daydreaming about a fantasy future or worrying about impending disasters? Did you hash and rehash past problems? Cling to regrets and resentments? How often were you fully alert to the present moment?

With abstinence, our time and attention can be devoted to the here and now. Instead of overeating to escape the anxiety we feel over whether or not we will be able to pay our bills, we can use the same amount of energy in productive work that will increase our income. We will never have perfect security, but we do not have to spoil today with worry about what we might not have tomorrow. The same power which sustains us now will be with us then.

In the same way, we do not have to worry now about how hungry we might be in the morning, or even later this afternoon. Next week's abstinence is not our problem now. All we have to do is follow the program in the present. We are learning that we can do practically anything if it is only for twenty-four hours! We can even be courteous to the people who exasperate us if we concentrate on being polite just for today.

Sinking deeply into the present moment makes us aware of a multitude of signals that we probably missed when we were overeating. When we focus on what is happening right now, in both our inner and outer worlds, we can react appropriately to whatever comes along. Instead of planning the next binge, we can extract a maximum amount of pleasure out of the sights, sounds, feelings, and ideas that are immediately at hand. Even unpleasant situations can be a means of growth when they are faced and experienced.

There are many interesting and challenging things to do when we are no longer obsessed with food and eating. We who have walked into a new life by means of O.A. and the Twelve Step program have been greatly blessed. Step Twelve is our on-going way of saying thank you. Of course, the most important help we can give to other compulsive overeaters is the maintenance of our own physical, emotional, and spiritual abstinence. Beyond this, each opportunity we take to spread the good news of the program enriches our shared recovery.